PUB WAL
IN
Northumberland

John Sadler

COUNTRYSIDE BOOKS
NEWBURY, BERKSHIRE

COUNTRYSIDE BOOKS
3 Catherine Road
Newbury, Berkshire

To view our complete range of books,
please visit us at
www.countrysidebooks.co.uk

ISBN 1 85306 976 0
EAN 978 1 85306 976 5

Dedicated to Hannah Wallis

The cover picture of Bamburgh was supplied by
Pictures of Britain (Mike Cowan)

Photographs by the author

Designed by Peter Davies, Nautilus Design
Produced through MRM Associates Ltd., Reading
Printed by Woolnough Bookbinding Ltd., Irthlingborough

Contents

Area Map Showing Location of the Walks

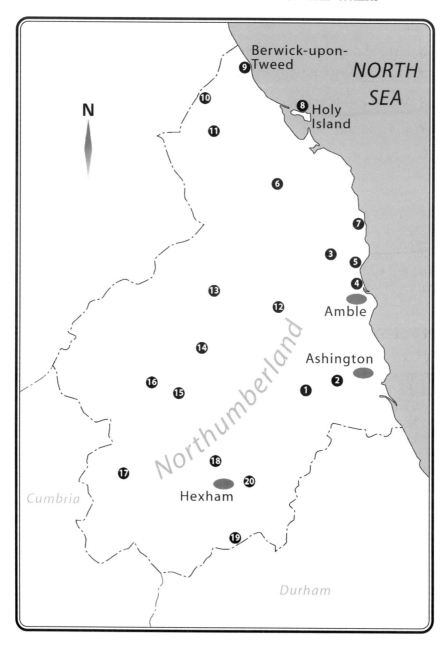

Walk

ACKNOWLEDGEMENTS

This book could not have been written without the assistance of the following people to whom my thanks are due: Alan Grint, Julia Young, Christine Browell and, of course, my wife Ruth, for her patience and good humour throughout.

PUBLISHER'S NOTE

We hope that you obtain considerable enjoyment from this book; great care has been taken in its preparation. However, changes of landlord and actual closures of pubs are sadly not uncommon. Likewise, although at the time of publication all routes followed public rights of way or permitted paths, diversion orders can be made and permissions withdrawn.

We cannot, of course, be held responsible for such diversion orders and any inaccuracies in the text which result from these or any other changes to the routes nor any damage which might result from walkers trespassing on private property. We are anxious though that all details covering the walks are kept up to date and would therefore welcome information from readers which would be relevant to future editions.

The simple sketch maps that accompany the walks in this book are based on notes made by the author whilst checking out the routes on the ground. However, for the benefit of a proper map, we do recommend that you purchase the relevant Ordnance Survey sheet covering your walk. The Ordnance Survey maps are widely available, especially through booksellers and local newsagents.

INTRODUCTION

Northumberland is one of the most unspoilt counties in England – there are miles of beautiful countryside, a wealth of history at every turn and some splendid pubs to visit.

There are the high upland dales of Coquetdale, Redesdale and Tynedale that run towards the border between England and Scotland; the long ribbon of the North Sea coast that boasts some of the finest beaches in these islands, a 'lordly strand' of tumbled dunes and sparkling sands which are invariably far from crowded and the high fell sandstone of the Cheviots and the valleys that merge into the softer margins of the coastal plain.

And, of course, there is Hadrian's Wall that sweeps majestically along the summit of the Whin Sill, and across long miles of ragged hills. The Wall, now a World Heritage Site, attracts some three quarters of a million tourists and walkers each year and two of the walks in this book allow you to sample a section of this dramatic Roman spectacle, with the opportunity to visit the famous Roman forts of Housesteads and Vindolanda.

There are also circuits around some of Northumberland's finest towns such as Alnwick, home to the famous gardens that have been laid out in the castle grounds; historic Morpeth; and Berwick, with its fine Elizabethan walls. Add to these, routes at Lindisfarne and past some of the great castles on the coast such as Bamburgh, Warkworth and Dunstanburgh, and you can get some idea of the treats in store.

Each walk can be combined with a stop at a good pub for refreshments and telephone numbers are included so you can check out the opening times and availability of food. The accompanying sketch maps are intended to guide you to the pub and give you a simple idea of the route to be followed. The numbers of the relevant Ordnance Survey maps are also included and it is recommended that you arm yourself with one to get the maximum enjoyment from your outing.

We must not forget that Northumberland is England's most northerly county and, as such, the weather can suddenly turn, so do follow the walker's motto 'Go prepared and you'll be spared'. This means that it is always sensible to carry waterproofs with you, even on the sunniest of days and wear sensible footwear – ideally a pair of walking boots. You will then be ready for whatever the weather brings.

So, it just remains for me to wish you many happy hours walking the paths of this superb county.

John Sadler

The Beresford Arms

A WALK THROUGH GENTLY UNDULATING COUNTRYSIDE TO THE PRETTY HAMLET OF OGLE, BEFORE RETURNING OVER THE RIVER BLYTH TO EXPLORE WHALTON, AN ATTRACTIVE AND HISTORIC MID-NORTHUMBERLAND VILLAGE, WITH A MOST INTERESTING MANOR HOUSE.

The area around Whalton is entirely rural, being outside the spread of the former south-east Northumberland coal field. It seems previously to have comprised a number of stout block houses or peles but these have all been replaced by pretty 19th-century cottages and some imposing larger houses. Of these, the manor house is the most notable, having been remodelled by the distinguished Edwardian architect, Sir Edwin Lutyens who also refurbished Lindisfarne Castle.

THE BERESFORD ARMS is a long-established inn with a pleasant ivy-clad façade. It is very much a village pub and its menu comprises a range of unpretentious starters such as soup, pâté, or prawn cocktail with, for main course, a choice of lamb, beef pie, scampi, salmon, duck and chicken dishes. In addition there is a good spread of puddings. The landlord also offers a weekday special three-course dinner menu for a reasonable cost. The bar hosts a range of draught and bottled beers, ciders and spirits, and wine can be bought 'on tap' by the glass.

Food is served daily from midday till 2.30 pm and, in the evenings, from 6 pm till 9 pm. Children are welcome and there is a pleasant garden area.

✆ 01670 775225.

How to get there: Whalton is about 3 miles to the east of Belsay and the pub is located in the centre of the village, on the left as you drive east on the A6087.

Parking: There is parking at the pub for patrons. There is also limited on-street parking in the village.

Length of the walk: 5 miles. Maps: OS Explorer 316 and 325 (GR 128815).

THE WALK

1 Leaving the pub car park, bear left in an easterly direction along the village street, passing the pleasing cottages and houses on your left. As you approach the end of the village street you will pass the manor house also on your left. This is a very fine Lutyens property which, even in its austere northern setting, has an 'arts and crafts' style to it. On approaching the left-hand bend of the A6087 as it heads out toward **Morpeth**, cross the road and join the narrow single-lane track that is marked '**Shilvington**'. Follow this for over a mile.

The road, lined on both sides with mature sycamore and

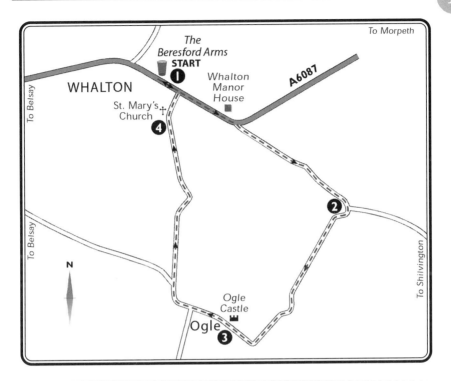

ash, dips and meanders in the gently undulating landscape and there is generally very little traffic.

You will pass, on your right-hand side, the lanes leading, firstly, to **North Low House** and then to **East and West Low Houses**. These are what might be called typical Northumbrian farms, quite long, double-storied, with small-paned sash windows, symmetrical and unpretentious.

2 After 1¼ miles, you arrive at a T-junction. Bear right in the direction of **Ogle**. The road remains narrow and, whereas before it twisted and turned, here it strikes southward, arrow straight, passing, on your right, **West House**. Continue in this direction for 1 mile or so. The way takes you over a charming hump-backed bridge before swinging right and westward toward the hamlet of Ogle. Ignoring the

St Mary in Walton

left-hand turning that would take you to the farm at **Bonas Hill**, continue on to **Ogle Castle** (a private residence), which dates from the reign of Charles I. Long before that, however, the place was a castle or 'fortalice' in the ownership of the Ogle family who lived in Northumberland even before the Norman Conquest. The village itself is charming and has won several awards for its well-tended gardens.

3 Keep going through the village, heading west, and at the end of the single row of properties the road bears right and is signposted to **Whalton**. Continue in this direction, heading downhill towards **Howburn Bridge** where you cross the **River Blyth. Whalton Dene House** and **Whalton Mill** are on your left. The road now climbs gradually toward **Whalton** itself and you approach the village from the south through a series of bends which take you past the school and then, immediately, the church on your left.

4 The **church of St Mary** is a fine Early English parish church, with Saxon traces, and it houses the 'Whalton Christ', an amazing montage that was created for the village's millennium festivities. When you reach the junction, turn left past the village hall and back to the pub.

PLACES OF INTEREST NEARBY

Belsay Hall and Gardens, on the A696 south-west of Whalton, have been lovingly restored by English Heritage. Telephone: 01661 881636.

The Waterford Lodge

THIS WALK BEGINS BY EXPLORING THE HISTORIC STREETS OF MORPETH, THEN TAKES YOU ON A STROLL ALONG THE BANKS OF THE RIVER WANSBECK AND A RAMBLE THROUGH DELIGHTFUL CARLISLE PARK TO THE ANCIENT REMAINS OF THE CASTLE. THERE ARE SOME GRADIENTS THAT MAY BE TACKLED BRAVELY UP THE STEPS PROVIDED OR MORE SEDATELY BY THE WINDING PATHS!

Morpeth is a pretty market town on the fringe of the old south-east Northumberland coalfield. It is essentially rural in character and was much 'visited' by predatory Scots during the long years of the border wars from 1296 to 1603. Carlisle Park is maintained by the local authority and is well known locally for the floral displays in spring and summer.

THE WATERFORD LODGE is an attractive former coaching inn, now a public house, hotel and restaurant. Situated on the south bank of the Wansbeck, the rambling exterior gives a clear indication of its heritage. Rendered and painted, the external elevations belie the interior which is more contemporary in style. There is a selection of food on offer including Italian pasta, and more traditional fare consists of starters such as garlic mushrooms, prawn cocktail and soups to be followed by scampi, cod, salmon and steaks. A traditional roast is available at Sunday lunchtime. In addition to an adequate wine list, the pub has a range of hand-pulled and bottled ales.

Food is normally served at lunchtime from 12 noon to 2 pm and in the evenings from 6 pm to 9 pm. Children are welcome and dogs are allowed in the bar area.

✆ 01670 512004.

How to get there: Morpeth is about 15 miles north of Newcastle, off the A1. The pub is located off the main street opposite the imposing castellated edifice of the Old Courthouse and Gaol as you drive into the town.

Parking: There is a small 'pay and display' car park directly in front of the pub, which does not have designated parking. If this is busy, use the town's large car park across the river.

Length of the Walk: 3 miles. Map: OS Explorer 325 (GR 201857).

THE WALK

1 From the front entrance of the **Waterford Lodge**, immediately bear right. Then, crossing the road, make for the cast-iron footbridge (the **Chantry Bridge**, erected in 1869) that spans the **Wansbeck**. Once over the bridge you will immediately see the remains of the medieval chantry on

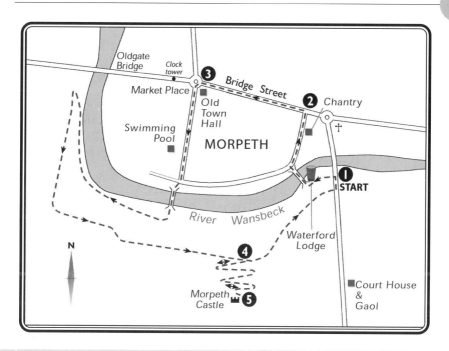

your right-hand side. This was originally the 13th-century **Chapel of All Saints** which, in 1552, became **Morpeth Grammar School** and many generations of scholars passed through its doors until 1845. The building now houses a craft exhibition, the tourist information office and the **Bagpipe Museum** - a unique collection of smallpipes, Irish, Scottish and other nations' bagpipes.

2 Bear left onto **Bridge Street,** a busy shopping thoroughfare, and continue till you reach the roundabout in front of the **Clock Tower.** Before you reach this you will pass the old town hall, an imposing building in a rather severe Baroque style. This was constructed in 1714 by the famous early Georgian architect, Vanbrugh. The Clock Tower itself was built around 1640 using medieval masonry. Up until 1802 the tower also served as the town lock up!

THE OLD COURT HOUSE AT MORPETH WAS BUILT IN 1881.

3 Turn left at the roundabout and walk towards another cast-iron span, **Elliot Bridge,** passing the swimming baths and leisure complex to your right. The bridge takes you once again to the south bank of the **Wansbeck** which sweeps around three sides of the town. Once over the river, turn right along its banks. This is a particularly pretty stretch of water, fringed by mature trees. Follow the gentle curve of the river as it bends west and northwards toward **Oldgate Bridge,** but before you get there the path forks very sharply to the left and you head due south, through the sheltering trees, as the ground rises.

At the Y-junction, branch left again, the path climbing gently upwards, and follow this along the crest of the shallow ridge that runs eastward and parallel to the river. Keep going past the steep ascent of the '100 steps' on your right and follow the sweep of the path till you see the conical mound of **Haw Hill** directly in front of you.

④ Now you descend as the path leads into the deep little valley between **Haw Hill** and the higher ground to the south crowned by the present castle. You can ascend either by the steep stairs or the more gentle zigzag pathway edged with willow wattles. The castle comprises the well preserved, much restored remains of the 14th-century gatehouse, with some traces of the earlier sections of curtain wall.

⑤ Retrace your steps down the hillside (much easier going down!) and follow the path at the bottom in an easterly direction. This leads you into the beautifully tended formal gardens of **Carlisle Park** and past a small aviary to the park entrance. Across the road is the **Old Court House**. This was constructed in the 1820s and was used as the gaol until 1881, then as the police station until 1939 and continued in use as a court until 1980. Still within the confines of the park and located to the right of the entrance is the garden clock presented to the townspeople in 1972 by James Fairbairn Smith of Detroit, in memory of the achievement of a former mayor, Alderman Bertram Jobson. Turn left from the park gates and walk the short distance back towards the **Waterford Lodge**.

PLACES OF INTEREST NEARBY

A couple of miles west of **Morpeth** is the delightful village of Mitford, with the ruin of **Mitford Castle** crowning the high ground above the village. The early Norman castle was burnt down by King John and a second castle was built on the site, this time including an unusual five-sided keep, thought to be the only such keep in Britain. It is the ruin of this exceptional keep that has been preserved.

The White Swan

From the moment you enter Alnwick through the medieval gate named after Sir Henry Percy, known as Hotspur because of his enthusiasm for fighting the Scots, you are aware of the ancient glories of these great magnates of the North. This fascinating walk visits the castle of the Percys before heading out from the town over the distinctive Lion Bridge and into the countryside. Pleasant parkland surrounds you and there are fine views and interesting historic remains to enjoy, before returning to Alnwick over the Canongate Bridge.

———————◆●◆———————

Alnwick is the ducal seat of the Percys, who have been a power in the region since they acquired the barony in the early 14th century. The town, most of which dates from the 19th century, is dominated by the great medieval castle. Still a formidable looking fortress, the walls were extensively altered in the Victorian era by Anthony Salvin, the celebrated architect, and the castle today is essentially a very grand country house with spectacular interiors and a fine armoury. In recent years the Duchess of Northumberland has developed the extensive gardens into a major regional attraction.

THE WHITE SWAN is a 17th-century coaching inn, located in the centre of Alnwick, near the medieval archway. It boasts 57 bedrooms and one of its suites of rooms is panelled with the wood from SS *Olympic*, sister ship to the ill-fated *Titanic*. A good range of bar meals is on offer in the bar lounge. There are traditional meat and fish dishes, with a variety of starters and puddings, together with sandwiches. Food is served throughout the week from 12 noon to 5.30 pm and from 6 pm to 9.30 pm.

In addition to the normal eating and drinking facilities, the hotel offers murder mystery weekends and other promotions. There is a wide selection of bar and main meals in the lounge known as Hardy's Bar, after the famous locally-based manufacturer of fishing rods. There is also a good restaurant with an extensive wine list and guest beers. Children are welcome but dogs are not permitted in the restaurant.

✆ 01665 602109.

How to get there: The White Swan is located centrally in Alnwick, which is easily accessible via the A1, approximately 30 miles north of Newcastle upon Tyne.

Parking: On-street car parking (metered) is available near the White Swan.

Length of the Walk: 3½ miles. The longer walk, past Heckley adds roughly a mile to your stroll. Map: OS Explorer 332 (GR 188135).

THE WALK

1 From the hotel, proceed through the centre of **Alnwick** towards the castle. On the way, you will pass the town hall, a fine five-bay block built in 1731 and the market place itself, which, if located in the south of the country, could be taken as a setting for a Thomas Hardy novel. The eastern flank of the market place is dominated by **Northumberland Hall** which dates from 1826. This is a much grander edifice than the town hall itself and has a very distinctive open arcaded ground floor.

Coming upon the castle, you will be impressed by the sheer size of the place. It dominates the town as effectively

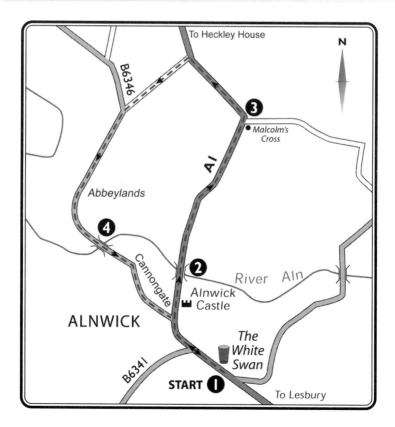

THE CASTLE AT ALNWICK

now as it would have done in medieval times. Note the distinctive stone figures commanding the battlements of the outer gateway or barbican.

2 From the castle, head north-east down toward the Lion Bridge. This wonderful span was built by John Adam in 1773 in the Gothick manner with the distinctive Percy Lion standing guard. As you cross over the **River Aln**, you gain a fine view of the castle and surrounding parkland. Follow the road as it leads uphill toward **Malcolm's Cross**, with the pleasant parkland of **North Demesne** on the right. On your left, you will pass the remains of St Leonard's, a medieval hospice. The cross itself, which stands inside Long Plantation, was erected to mark the alleged spot where Malcolm III, King of the Scots was killed in 1093.

3 Turn left and northward along what used to be the old A1 which, nowadays, is a tranquil byway. Pass **Loaning Head** on your left, then turn left onto **Smiley Lane** before you reach **Heckley**.

If you wish to take the longer route, continue past Heckley to Heckley House, then bear left toward Heckley High

House which brings you down to Smiley Lane Cottage and back onto the main route.

Continue south-west past **Abbeylands** and the abbey remains which are on your right as the roads swings southward.

(4) Recross the **River Aln** by the **Canongate Bridge**. The area on your left is **Hulne Park,** crowned in the distance by the rise of **Brizlee Hill** and the celebrated **Brizlee Tower,** built around 1780, probably to a design by Robert Adam and a wonderful flourish of pure theatre in the Gothick style. Continue along the road till you find yourself once again approaching the castle square. On your right as you stroll along the pleasant terrace is the town museum, which houses some impressive arms and armour from the heyday of the border reivers. You will also pass the **Percy Tenantry column** which was constructed by local architect David Stephenson in 1816, and which rises to some 75 feet. Retrace your steps back to your car.

PLACES OF INTEREST NEARBY

Alnwick has been put very much on the visitor map recently by the opening of the Duchess of Northumberland's Garden which adjoins the castle. The gardens have won international recognition and have proved to be one of the most successful new U.K. tourist destinations. Telephone: 01665 511350.

The Hermitage Inn

THIS WALK BEGINS IN ONE OF THE COUNTY'S PRETTIEST VILLAGES BEFORE HEADING TOWARDS THE COAST FOR A STROLL ALONG THE LORDLY STRAND OF SHORE TOWARDS ALNMOUTH. IT THEN TURNS INLAND TO EXPLORE THE AREA AROUND SHORTRIDGE HALL AND HOUNDEAN MILL BEFORE RETURNING TO WARKWORTH, WITH THE OPPORTUNITY TO VISIT ITS IMPRESSIVE CASTLE.

The great architectural historian, Sir Nikolaus Pevsner describes the approach to Warkworth from the north as offering one of the most exciting sequences of views possible in England. The visitor's first glimpse is of the bridge, the medieval bridge tower and then the pleasing uphill curve of Bridge Street.

THE HERMITAGE INN dates from around 1760 and was originally built as a farm and local alehouse. Patrons probably had to share certain areas with the livestock, though I suspect neither would have complained! The present layout dates from the 1970s and comprises several comfortable lounge and bar areas, with traditional features such as stone-flagged floors.

A good range of bar meals and sandwiches is available, served on weekdays and at weekends from 12 noon to 2 pm and from 7 pm to 9 pm. The fare consists of traditional meat and fish dishes, with some curries and a good range of sandwiches; vegetarians are also catered for. Children are welcome and dogs permitted in the bar.

✆ 01665 711258.

How to get there: Warkworth lies on the A1068 north of Amble. The Hermitage Inn is at the north end of Bridge Street.

Parking: There is limited parking in the village itself with some bays at the north end of Bridge Street in front of the church. The castle field offers ample parking for English Heritage visitors and there is parking toward the links. The village can get busy at weekends and during holiday periods.

Length of the walk: 5 miles. OS Explorer 332 (GR 248057).

THE WALK

① From the pub, turn right down **Bridge Street**, veering right towards the tower and bridge. The street comprises some very fine 18th- and 19th-century town houses and opposite the pub stands the **Market Cross**, with beyond that **Dial Place** leading you to the church. The **church of St Lawrence** is well worth a detour. It is of Norman construction with some fine features. It was here in the 12th century that the

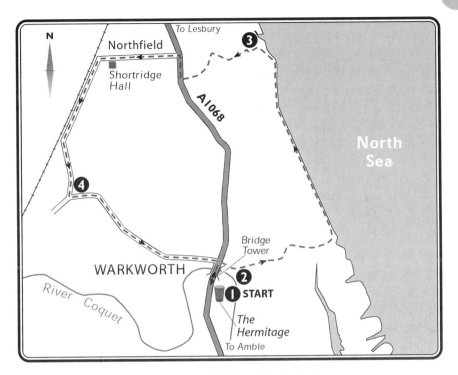

Scottish king, William the Lion, burned the entire congregation alive before he was defeated and captured at Alnwick.

2 Go over the bridge and take the single-lane road past the links towards the beach. The bridge, with its defensive tower, was constructed in the late 14th century and is one of the very few surviving fortified bridges in Britain. Pass through the dunes (there are public toilets provided at the end of the lane) and walk along the beach for just over a mile. If you look behind to the south, you'll see **Amble** harbour and marina, with **Coquet Island** lying offshore whilst, to the north, past **Birling Carrs** you can catch a glimpse of **Alnmouth** and the **Mardon Rocks** beyond.

(3) Once around the point, leave the shoreline to strike inland, over the steep tussocky slope of the dunes toward **Northfield**. Then follow the track, heading west, away from the coast till you reach the A1068 road. This is a busy highway and care needs to be taken. Turn right, and very soon cross over to take the lane toward **Shortridge Hall**. At the hall the road veers sharply left to head south, parallel to the main railway line.

(4) At **Houndean Mill** turn sharp left to walk back toward the north end of **Warkworth**. At the junction with the main road, turn right to cross the bridge where you began. Before returning to your car, however, you might like to walk up to the top of Bridge Street where a footpath on the west side takes you past the great bulk of the castle wall and offers you a marvellous view over the loop and swell of the River Coquet. Warkworth Castle, with its eight-towered keep, was once home to the powerful Percy family and unlike Alnwick or Bamburgh was not turned into a country house once its fighting days were over.

PLACES OF INTEREST NEARBY

Whilst in Warkworth make time to visit the **Hermitage**, in the care of English Heritage. This is a remarkable chapel and sacristy carved from the living rock sometime around 1330, in an extraordinarily beautiful and romantic location. It is reached by following the river path below the castle for approximately ¼ mile then crossing the river by rowing boat, an experience which imparts a particular magic to the visit. Telephone: 01665 711423.

The Schooner Hotel

THIS WALK TAKES YOU FROM ALNMOUTH, IN ITS MAGNIFICENT COASTAL SETTING, TO FOLLOW THE CURVE OF THE RIVER ALN THROUGH THE VILLAGES OF LESBURY AND HIPSBURN BEFORE RETURNING TO ENJOY MORE WONDERFUL VIEWS OVER THE ESTUARY.

The former port of Alnmouth lies, as its name suggests, on the sweep of the Aln estuary facing a picturesque shoreline. It was built in medieval times to serve the great Percy fortress of Alnwick, a few miles upstream. Over centuries the port declined and the town became a 19th-century spa. It still retains a feeling of slightly faded gentility.

THE SCHOONER HOTEL is at the southern end of the main thoroughfare on the right, a pleasant white-painted structure that blends perfectly into the traditional but rather eclectic mix. Originally a coaching inn, it is distinguished by its numerous resident ghosts, most notoriously that of Parson Smythe!

There are a couple of comfortable lounge bars and a large rear conservatory, decorated in a homely manner. The pub serves a range of locally brewed ales. There is an excellent bar menu with traditional meat and fish options, plus a vegetarian choice, and food is served daily from 12 noon to 9 pm. Children are welcome and dogs permitted in the bar.

☎ 01665 830216.

How to get there: From the A1 branch onto the A1068 towards Alnmouth, turning onto the B1338 into the town.
Parking: The Schooner is on the main street and there are some parking areas nearby, though the town can be busy in peak times.
Length of the walk: 3½ miles. OS Explorer 332 (GR 245105).

THE WALK

1 From the **Schooner**, go north along the line of **Northumberland Street**, which runs like the backbone of a whale across the promontory on which **Alnmouth** stands. Leave the village and head north by the minor road that follows the coast. The golf links will be on your right crowding against the shore line. Continue past **Marden House** and **Foxton Hall**, all to your left.

2 Beyond **Foxton** you arrive at a T-junction where you bear left toward **Lesbury**. You will arrive in the village after not quite 1 mile. Carry on towards the T-junction with the main road. Pass **St Mary's church** which, though much rebuilt in

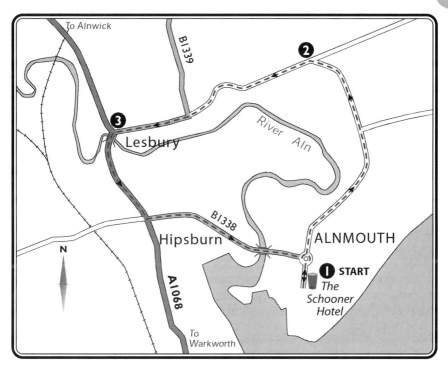

the 19th century, is an Early English foundation. The vicarage and nearby Lesbury House also date from the 19th century but the bridge over the Aln is much earlier, probably 15th-century. It's worth looking to your right when you reach the junction, to see the well-constructed and elegant viaduct that dates from c.1850. It was designed by the celebrated local engineer Robert Stephenson, son of George Stephenson, the railway pioneer.

As you look over toward the sweep of coastline to the east, with the tumbling dunes and inviting sands, it is worth recalling that smuggling was rife on this stretch of coast during the 18th and 19th centuries. Much of it was centred on the inn at nearby Boulmer. Isaac Addison, its most celebrated landlord, was commonly known as Isaac the Smuggler!

ALNMOUTH WAS A SPA TOWN IN THE 19TH CENTURY.

3 At the junction turn left, heading south toward **Hipsburn**. This is a relatively modern settlement clustering around Alnmouth station. At Hipsburn bear left again onto the B1338, that takes you back into **Alnmouth**. Cross the **Duchess's Bridge** dating from 1864 and turn right down **Northumberland Street** to return to your starting point.

PLACES OF INTEREST NEARBY

The great fortress of **Alnwick** lies only a few miles upstream from the Aln Estuary. This imposing medieval castle has been used for several film locations, including being featured as Hogwarts in the first two Harry Potter films. Telephone: 01665 510777.

The Percy Arms

A LEVEL WALK THROUGH COUNTRYSIDE THAT ABOUNDS WITH MYSTERIOUS PREHISTORIC REMAINS, WITH AN OPTIONAL VISIT TO THE FAMOUS CASTLE AT CHILLINGHAM AND ITS WONDERFUL GARDENS.

Chatton is what is termed a 'model' village, one that was 'improved' by the Duke of Northumberland in the mid-19th century. It is hard to believe now, but prior to this many villagers lived in damp and insanitary medieval cottages, a breeding ground for diseases such as typhus and tuberculosis that regularly ravaged the rural population. The attractive village today consists of a range of Tudor-style cottages, a post office and the blacksmith's forge.

THE PERCY ARMS, in Chatton, is a pleasant country inn with an L-shaped bar and an open fire, a welcome addition in winter. The pub serves a good range of bar meals, snacks and sandwiches. There is an excellent choice of meat, fish and game dishes, with vegetarian options, and food is served daily from 12 noon to 2 pm and from 6.30 pm to 9.30 pm. Children are welcome and dogs are permitted in certain areas.
✆ 01668 215244.

How to get there: Chatton lies on the B6348, just east of Wooler. The pub will be found toward the western end of the main street.

Parking: There is ample free car parking around the pub and in the village.

Length of the walk: 5½ miles (a detour to the castle, which is highly recommended, would add another mile to the walk). OS Explorer 340 (GR 055284).

THE WALK

1 From the pub turn right and then immediately left to head south toward **Chillingham**. The bridge that crosses the meandering course of the **River Till** dates from the early 18th century. Carry on into **Chillingham**.

If you wish to visit Chillingham castle, turn left to the entrance. There has been a castle here since the 13th century though the present medieval core is from around the mid-14th century. The present owner, Sir Humphrey Wakefield, acquired the estate in the 1980s and has worked tirelessly to restore it to its former glory. The gardens are extensive. After your visit, retrace your steps to the main road. Carry on southward along the main road till you reach the junction at **West Lodge**.

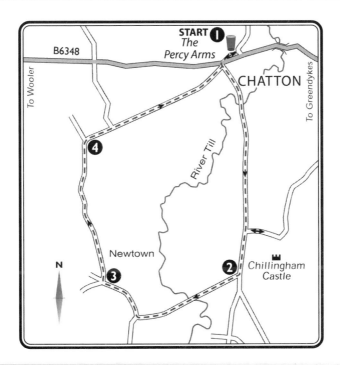

2 Turn right toward **Newtown** (about 1 mile). Again you will cross the wandering course of the **Till**, this time by **Newtown Bridge**. As you approach the Y-junction where you turn right to Newtown, you bisect the line of the **Devil's Causeway**, the old Roman road. The immediate area abounds with prehistoric remains. Past the hamlet of Newtown you head north-west for under ½ mile till you reach a further Y-junction at **Knock Well**.

3 Here you take the right fork for a straight stretch of over a mile. The going is easy and the scenery pleasant. To your left is **Pond** and then **Howemoor Plantation** and there are ancient remains of hut circles and enclosures. As **Trickley Wood** angles toward the road from your left, the main branch of the road veers sharply right at **Ferny Law**.

4 You are now heading north-east, back towards **Chatton**. The road again is straight, the distance over 1 mile and, halfway, you'll pass the farm at Broomhouse on your left. The road leads you straight back into the village.

CHILLINGHAM CASTLE NEAR CHATTON HAS UNDERGONE MUCH RESTORATION.

PLACES OF INTEREST NEARBY

Chillingham Castle is undoubtedly the main visitor attraction in the immediate area. It is open most afternoons except Saturdays from May to September. Telephone: 01668 215359.

The wild cattle in the grounds are also unique. They can be viewed but not approached – wild, in this case means just that!

Chatton Sandyfords, east of the village by Chatton Moor, offers several prehistoric burial sites and a group of the mysterious incised rocks known as cup and ring stones. They probably date to around 2000 BC.

The Jolly Fishermen

THE MAGNIFICENT SHELL OF MIGHTY DUNSTANBURGH CASTLE DOMINATES THIS WALK ALONG THE SPECTACULAR COASTLINE NORTH OF CRASTER, A PRETTY FORMER FISHING VILLAGE. THE ROUTE THEN BRINGS YOU AWAY FROM THE SHORE NORTHWARD PAST THE GOLF COURSE, THROUGH DUNSTAN STEADS AND OVER LEVEL GROUND BACK TOWARD THE VILLAGE.

Craster is a very pretty and extremely popular former fishing village. Tourism has replaced fishing as the staple industry and many of the former fishermen's cottages are now holiday homes. The village is renowned for the famous Craster kippers that are still produced in the 19th-century smoke house.

THE JOLLY FISHERMAN, which dates from 1847, has spectacular views over the North Sea and is a popular pub. The atmosphere is friendly and informal, and children are welcome (as are dogs but on the lower floor only). The cosy bar areas are complemented by open fires. Seafood is a speciality and food is served daily, on Sundays and weekdays from 11 am to 8 pm, with a good bar menu and sandwiches. Its crab sandwiches and kipper pâté made from the produce of the smoke house are renowned. There is a good choice of ales and a small selection of wines.

  ∅ 01665 576461.

How to get there: The village is reached from the A1 via the B1340. The Jolly Fisherman is on the right of the harbour past the smoke house.
Parking: The main car park (pay and display) is just as you come into the village by the tourist information centre. This can get busy at peak times.
Length of the walk: 4½ miles. OS Explorer 332 (GR 257195).

THE WALK

1 From the **Jolly Fisherman** walk down to the harbour. Continue along the path that leads past a row of houses until you reach the gate that faces directly towards the castle about a mile away, brooding over the flat coastal lands.

2 Proceed now along the coastal path with the rocky foreshore on your right. The stretch of coast as you leave the village is known as the **Little Carr**, nearer the castle it becomes **Cushat Steer.**

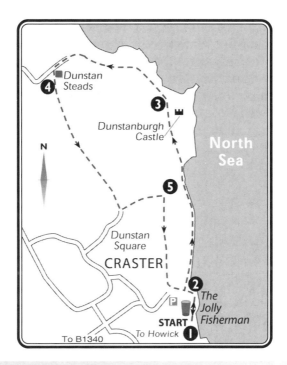

As you walk on, the castle gradually looms larger and larger till it comes to fill the horizon. On the northern elevation, facing the coast toward Castle Point, the cliffs are so spectacularly steep that no defensive walls were needed and the total area of some 11 acres, enclosed by defences, makes this the largest castle in Northumberland. The great fortress has been a favoured subject for several generations of artists including, perhaps most famously, Turner. It was built by Thomas, Earl of Lancaster in the early 14th century.

3 The walk continues to the north of the castle, past the solitary finger of **Lilburn's Tower** as the path skirts the fringe of the **Dunstanburgh Castle Golf Course**. Do refrain from straying onto the links and watch out for flying golf balls! Birdwatchers can look forward to seeing fulmar, kittiwake, razorbill and eider, which breed in the shelter of the cliffs. The seaward views are spectacular, looking over the **Greymare Rock** toward **Embleton Bay**. It is not surprising that this coastline was once popular with French privateers and local smugglers.

4 As you angle inland toward **Dunstan Steads Farm,** you pass through the farmyard and then turn sharply left and southward on the concrete road that will lead you to **Dunstan Square Farm**. From here you turn left heading back toward the coast, though **Scrog Hill** stands between you and the castle. The path, which can be indistinct, runs in the shadow of the whinstone ridge on which the castle sits.

5 At the kissing gate turn right and head south back towards **Craster**. The path will bring you out on the road before it enters the village. Turn left onto the tarmac and proceed back to your starting point.

PLACES OF INTEREST NEARBY

The great, ruined castle of **Dunstanburgh** (owned by the National Trust but in the care of English Heritage) was one of the main coastal defences against Scottish inroads and the gatehouse keep is of particular interest. Telephone: 01665 576231.

The Crown & Anchor Inn

A WALK AROUND THE MAGICAL ISLAND THAT HAS BEEN A SACRED SITE SINCE THE EARLY CHRISTIAN PERIOD IS AN EXPERIENCE NOT TO BE MISSED. THE VAST SWEEP OF SILVERED SANDS STRETCH TO THE HORIZON, WITH ONLY THE CASTLE ROCK TO BREAK THE SKYLINE.

Lindisfarne – Holy Island – is not truly an island, surrounded by sea. It becomes so only at high tide when the causeway is flooded by the ebb and suck of the swift moving currents. Visitors should take care to check the safe crossing times daily before making the journey. Lindisfarne was one of the first footholds that the Saxons gained on the Northumbrian coast and by the end of the 8th century it had become a flourishing monastic community. Today the ecclesiastical ruins remain a place of pilgrimage. The village itself is unique, a delightful mix of buildings, characterised by a riot of pantiled roofs. The main thoroughfare is Marygate and St Oswald's, the last house on the way up to the castle, is said to be the design of Sir Edwin Lutyens, who worked on the castle itself in the early 20th century. Around the harbour you will see a number of old fishermen's stores constructed by the simple expedient of overturning redundant fishing boats or cobles. These Dickensian features were often used as habitations during the 19th century.

THE CROWN & ANCHOR is superbly located in the very centre of the historic village, with magnificent views and only a stone's throw from the church and priory. It would be easy to imagine the ghosts of past fishermen crowding the bar with tales from the cold offshore waters, whose treacherous rocks and currents have claimed many ships and very many lives! It offers a good bar menu and sandwiches – crab is a speciality – from 12 noon to 2.15 pm weekdays and on Sundays and also from 6.30 pm to 8.30 pm on weekdays. It features a fine selection of ales and spirits, together with a wine list. Children are welcome in the restaurant.
℘ 01289 307454.

How to get there: Lindisfarne is easily accessible from the main A1 as it heads north to Berwick upon Tweed. The island is reached via the causeway. This is passable only at low tide so do check safe crossing times (telephone: 01670 533000). The causeway looks deceptive at low tide with the rolling flats around, but the tide comes in very quickly indeed.
Parking: There is a large 'pay and display' car park as you are about to enter the village.
Length of the walk: 5½ miles. OS Explorer 340 (GR 132422). The walking is along coastal paths and the foreshore, and so rocky surfaces can be slippery when wet.

THE WALK

1 From the car park head for the shoreline but turn right before you progress that far. At the marker, pass through the gate and take the path into the nature reserve.

You are following in the footsteps of St Aidan who arrived here from Iona in AD 635 at the invitation of King Oswald, who had restored Christianity to Northumbria. When the saint died in 651 a young shepherd named Cuthbert witnessed a vision of Aidan's soul ascending to Heaven. Inspired by his experience the youth sought holy orders and, in due course, came to Lindisfarne. St Cuthbert became the greatest Northumbrian saint, whose sacred banner witnessed victory over the Scots at Northallerton in 1138, at Falkirk in 1298 and at Neville's Cross in 1346.

2 When the path forks, keep going toward the dunes and pass

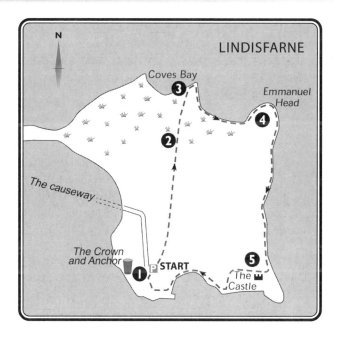

THE PRIORY AT LINDISFARNE.

the lime kilns. This complex of kilns, dating from the 1860s, is one of the largest in the county. At the rear there are traces of the railway line that transported the stone to the kilns from quarries on the other side of the island. Having inspected the kilns, keep on towards the shore, passing through the dunes.

3 Follow the shore, bearing to your right and you will round **Snipe Point** to enter **Coves Bay**. Walk around the head of the cove on the pleasant sands making toward the bluffs at the

further edge (at high tide it may be necessary to follow the path above the beach). Once you have rounded **Castlehead Rocks,** you will have an easy and pleasant stroll along the flat shore line toward the navigation marker on **Emmanuel Head.**

4 It is at this point that you bear slightly inland following the dunes toward the castle on its rocky perch.

The backdrop stretches to lordly Bamburgh and the remote Farne Islands, where the saints withdrew to contemplate in total isolation. The castle on Beblowe Crag began life as an artillery outpost in the reign of Henry VIII and the rock on which it stands is another outcrop of the whin sill that elsewhere bears the weight of Hadrian's Wall as well as Bamburgh and Dunstanburgh.

5 From the castle, walk down the lane back toward the village but turn left into the harbour itself. Once you reach the pier, bear right to ascend the **Heugh.** This was the site of a small fort erected in the late 17th century and you continue right past the lookout, the **Lutyens war memorial** and the remains of the **Lantern Chapel.** Once over the Heugh, follow the rising track on the right which brings you to **St Mary's church** and the **Priory** complex beyond. The parish church, which is looked after by Franciscans, is mainly of Early English construction. The Priory church is an epic ruin, resonant with the echoes of a vanished monasticism. Leave the church to retrace your steps through the village back to the car park.

PLACES OF INTEREST NEARBY

Nearby is the great soaring fortress of **Bamburgh**, possibly Sir Lancelot's castle, the seat of the ancient Saxon kings of Northumbria and a prime defence against the Scots. It was extensively refurbished in the late 19th century by Lord Armstrong. Telephone: 01668 214515.

The King's Arms

THIS WALK IS AROUND THE ELIZABETHAN WALLS OF THE HISTORIC TOWN OF BERWICK, ARGUABLY THE FINEST WALLS OF THEIR KIND IN BRITAIN, IF NOT IN EUROPE. THE ROUTE AVOIDS TRAFFIC AND OFFERS VIEWS OVER THE TOWN AND THE RIVER TWEED, WHILE THE REMAINS OF THE CASTLE AND THE 18TH-CENTURY BARRACKS ARE WELL WORTH SEEING.

Berwick upon Tweed is an ancient town and was once Scotland's major port with a flourishing overseas trade. Then, in 1296, Edward I of England, 'Longshanks', invaded, intending to chastise his rebellious vassal, the Scottish King John. Berwick soon felt England's wrath. The citizens manned their inadequate defences and, unwisely, heaped insult on the besiegers. The town was taken by storm and a holocaust of murder, arson and pillage ensued. This outrage rather set the tone for the next three centuries and Berwick changed hands no fewer than 14 times until Richard of Gloucester (later Richard III) won it back for England in 1482.

The Elizabethan town walls consist of a series of massive corner fortifications or bastions, linked by stretches of wall. Earth redoubts and outworks crowded beyond the line of the walls, seeking to deny any attacker a vantage point for setting up his batteries of siege guns. The walls were never seriously tested though the town remained an important garrison. Today the walker can enjoy an uninterrupted stroll around the old town boundaries.

THE KING'S ARMS is located on Hide Hill, in the heart of Berwick. It is on your left as you walk down the hill, with the old town hall to your rear. A former coaching inn with an impressive façade, dating mainly from the 18th century, the hotel retains a number of period features whilst offering a very up-to-date choice of eating facilities. 'Il Porto di Mare', its Italian restaurant, offers a typical pizzeria-style menu and is open during normal restaurant hours, including most lunchtimes. For those wishing for a taste of the exotic but on the lighter side, a pavement café and bistro adjoins the restaurant. If a more traditional British approach to cooking is preferred, the garden terrace offers a wide range of light meals, a children's menu and, in summer, the chance to eat out in the old walled garden. A comprehensive wine list is available and there are 36 letting rooms, including family rooms and several with four posters! Meals are usually served from 12 noon to 2 pm and from 5 pm onwards.

☎ 01289 307454.

How to get there: From Newcastle the A1 heads directly north to Berwick. Follow the Berwick exit road to the bridge. Once over the bridge turn right at the mini roundabout down Marygate, past the old town hall and right again onto Hide Hill.

Parking: There are several adjacent car parks – the easiest to reach is that which lies immediately through the gates at the base of Hide Hill on the quayside.

Length of the walk: 3 miles, or 2 miles by keeping only to the circuit of the walls. OS Explorer 346 (GR 998533).

THE WALK

1 From the hotel, turn left to walk down **Hide Hill** till you reach the **Shoregate** and there ascend the stone stairs to the wall walk. Head right, along the line of the ramparts, walking in a north-westerly direction. The **Tweed**, fat and swollen at high tide, flows at the base of the walls. You are now on part of the original medieval walls, the newer construction of Queen Elizabeth's reign faced the more vulnerable northern and seaward flanks.

2 This section of the Quay Walls provides an excellent view of the 17th-century bridge and the landward side is crowded with pleasant 19th-century properties, including the former customs house. Modernity intrudes only briefly when you cross the road and then follow the steepening incline upward and under the span of the more recent bridge. **Meg's Mount** is the first bastion that you reach, dominating the land to the north, and you can clearly see why the Italian engineers charged with designing the circuit of the walls chose this as their defensive line. A bastion is like a low squat tower, intended to hold cannon.

For those who wish to do the longer walk, it is possible to

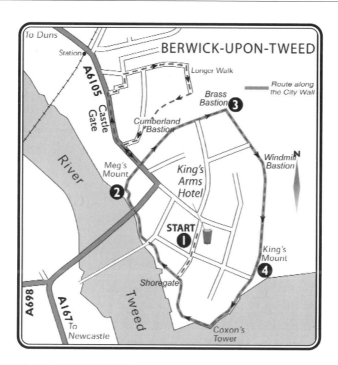

descend from the walls by **Meg's Mount** and pass through **Marygate** northward via **Castlegate**. This follows a curve around to the station and beyond. Just off Castle Terrace, a path leads down past the surviving section of the old castle walls to the **Watergate** by the river, with the magnificent arches of the **Royal Border Bridge** soaring above you. You can then follow the riverside path back to rejoin the circuit of the walls below Meg's Mount and continue.

From **Meg's Mount**, walk eastward along the Elizabethan walls. These are massively thick, relatively low, reinforced with tons of earth to resist the weight of a besieger's shot. Ramps were built to facilitate hauling the defenders' guns to the ramparts. The **Cumberland bastion** is located centrally on this northern section of the walls, with the **Brass Bastion** on the seaward flank. Here the circuit of the walls turns south – the waters of the North Sea before you. Despite the ravages of time and subsequent developments, many traces of the original outer works can still be made out.

3 On the landward side you will pass the unique **Cromwellian church**, one of the very few to have been built in the austere epoch of the Puritan Commonwealth, and also the sprawl of the 18th-century barracks designed by Vanbrugh, with Ravensdowne Hospital beyond. The next of the great bastions is the **Windmill**, which dominates the seaward side.

4 As you continue your walk southward, you will arrive at the **King's Mount**, the last of the great Elizabethan works, which overlooks the pier and the old harbour area. Just prior to the bastion, on the landward side, is the squat strength of the 18th-century magazine. Looking inland from the Mount, you're above the old town with some very pleasing Georgian buildings, a few of which are built right up to the walls themselves. The walk continues around the river estuary, where the mud flats are habitat for a variety of sea birds at low tide, and passes by Fisher's Fort and **Coxon's Tower** to return to the stairs above Shoregate. From the walls, retrace your steps back to the King's Arms.

PLACES OF INTEREST NEARBY

Why not travel south along the coast and explore the long sandy beaches at **Goswick**, complete with Second World War gun emplacements. Here, on fine days, the light dances on the great expanse of golden sand. Or, you could head for the spectacular coastline to the north of Berwick, towards **Eyemouth**, which has plunging cliffs sweeping down to the narrow shore – a smugglers' paradise!

The Masons Arms

THE CASTLE AT NORHAM HAS BEEN CALLED THE 'QUEEN OF BORDER FORTRESSES' AND THIS LOVELY WALK TOUCHES THE VERY BOUNDARY WITH SCOTLAND ON THE BANKS OF THE RIVER TWEED, BEFORE LEADING YOU ALONG THE RIVER, BENEATH AN IMPRESSIVE RAILWAY VIADUCT THAT IS A SMALLER VERSION OF THE GREAT ROYAL BORDER BRIDGE AND BACK TO NORHAM WITH ITS LARGE VILLAGE GREEN.

Norham has a particularly spacious feel, with a ribbon of pleasant streets around and away from the green. The surrounding area, Norhamshire, was formerly in the ownership of the Bishops of Durham. These Prince Bishops were great landowners and lay magnates during the Middle Ages and the great square keep of Norham stood guard over a vital crossing of the Tweed. Norham is the setting for Scott's epic poem *Marmion* and enough of the massive square keep and outer walls remain to provide an excellent impression of the strength of the defences. In the 19th century the Kelso section of the York, Newcastle and Berwick Railway ran nearby on an impressive viaduct over the River Tweed.

THE MASONS ARMS is a traditional pub, prettily situated not far from the extensive village green. It is a typical Northumbrian village inn, many of which are as yet untouched by the effects of mass tourism. It is welcoming and unpretentious, with a good range of traditional bar meals and sandwiches. Meals are served from 12 noon to 2 pm Sundays and weekdays; there is no food served on Sunday evenings but on weekdays meals are available from 7 pm to 8.30 pm. Children are welcome and dogs are allowed in the bar. ✆ 01289 382326.

How to get there: Norham can be reached either from the main A1 via the A698 or from the west via Cornhill on Tweed.
Parking: There is ample room to park in the village.
Length of the Walk: 4½ miles. OS Explorer 346 (GR 904473).

THE WALK

① From the **Masons Arms** walk left, in an easterly direction, till you reach the green and then bear left along **Pedwell Way** which leads you to the **parish church of St Cuthbert** – the most venerable of Northumbrian saints. This large, possibly Norman, church was extensively rebuilt during the 1830s. The size and scale of the building suggest links with the

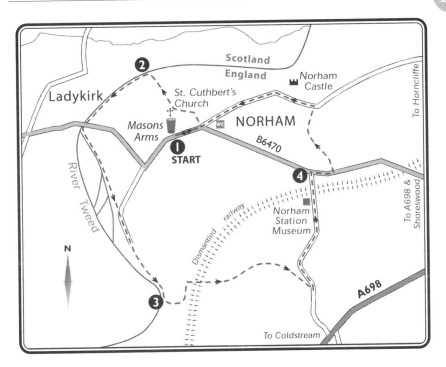

Prince Bishops. Your route takes you by the clearly-defined grassed pathway through the graveyard and then around and behind the north of the church. Here you will find a stile that leads you down to the **River Tweed**. You stand poised on the border itself for Scotland lies on the far side.

2 Follow the river bank to the left, heading upstream till you arrive at **Ladykirk** and Norham Bridge. This was constructed for the Tweed Bridges Trust in 1885-1887 to replace a previous, less robust crossing and is one of the most recent large stone bridges built in the county. Cross a further stile to your left, bear right and follow the field boundary. This takes you toward Bow Well Farm. Look for yet another stile which leads you down a wooded depression and into a small lane. Keep to your right and make for the

NORHAM CASTLE HAS UNDERGONE SUBSTANTIAL
CONSERVATION WORK.

gate marked 'Twizell Bridge'. Maintain your direction, following the course of the river.

3   You will come to a split in the path by a footbridge. Turn left and then, just a little way on, left again. As you reach the high point of the wooded area you will veer right to pass Newbiggin Dean and pass beneath one of the six high arches of the railway viaduct built in about 1850. It is a much smaller version of the great Royal Border Bridge and is attributed to Robert Stephenson. Now look for a junction over a further stile where you bear right at the sign for '**East Biggin**'. This pathway leads you out onto a lane and you turn left, ascending a gradient. After passing between the ruined pillars of another railway bridge you arrive at the station. Norham is the best surviving example of a Victorian

railway station on this section of the old line, designed in 1851 by Benjamin Green. The line vanished in the closures of the 1960s but happily the buildings have been preserved as a railway museum. Telephone: 01289 382217 for opening times.

4 Bear right at the end of the lane onto the B6470 but then look out for the bridleway on the other side of the road that takes you toward **Norham Castle**. Walk down to the bottom corner of this first field where you'll find a wooded track running by a stream. Very soon bear left over a footbridge into a second field where you veer right following the boundary till it leads you to the secondary road that runs by the front of the castle.

If you wish to detour into the site, it is in the care of English Heritage and has recently undergone substantial conservation. Even in its ruinous state one elevation of the massive stone keep survives as do significant stretches of the curtain walls of the inner and outer wards. It was attacked time and again by the Scots; once it was besieged for nearly two years. The last great attack, launched by James IV of Scotland at the start of his ill-fated Flodden expedition in 1513, saw the castle's ageing walls crumble before the roar of the great cannon and the fortress fell after an investment of only five days.

When you leave the castle, all that now remains is to walk down the hill back to the village and the **Masons Arms**, which you now approach from the east.

PLACES OF INTEREST NEARBY

Norham Castle is in the care of English Heritage and has a superb location overlooking the Tweed. The great square stone keep is one of the largest in the county and the place remained a stout bastion against the Scots (yes them again), for centuries! Telephone: 01289 382329.

The Black Bull

THIS PEACEFUL RURAL CIRCUIT IS FULL OF REMINDERS OF THE GREAT BATTLE OF FLODDEN FIELD, WHEN THE FLOWER OF THE SCOTTISH NOBILITY WAS SLAUGHTERED BY THE ENGLISH IN 1513. THE RIVER TILL ACCOMPANIES THE WALK TO FORD VILLAGE AND BACK TO ETAL, WHERE YOU CAN VISIT THE IMPRESSIVE CASTLE. THE ROUTE DOES INVOLVE CROSSING A FORD WHICH, AFTER HEAVY RAIN, MIGHT PROVE IMPASSABLE. SHOULD THIS BE THE CASE, A SHORTER, ALTERNATIVE WALK CAN BE FOLLOWED TO FORD CASTLE (SEE POINT 1 BELOW).

❦

Etal is often described as one of the most picturesque of Northumbrian villages, though in appearance it differs quite considerably, with several houses having whitewashed walls and an abundance of thatch. Most of the present buildings were erected by the then Lord Joicey in 1907 and replaced the poor quality dwellings of the medieval village. The castle, currently in the care of English Heritage, is a fine example of a 14th-century smaller castle or 'fortalice'. Together with neighbouring Ford, Etal was taken and burned by the Scots during James IV's campaign of 1513. The English were fully revenged in the great slaughter on Flodden Field nearby, when the pride of the Scottish army was cut to pieces and James IV and the bulk of the Scots nobility fell.

THE BLACK BULL is a traditional village pub, that is itself whitewashed and thatched. It serves a good range of ales and a wine list is available. The food is plentiful, with an emphasis on meat and game dishes, accompanied by a selection of vegetables. Food is served in the bar area every day during the summer from 12 noon to 8.45 pm. Children are welcome and dogs are allowed in the bar area.
   ✆ 01890 820200.

How to get there: From the A697 between Wooler and Cornhill-on-Tweed turn onto the B6353, and then onto the B6354 which, after a further mile or so, brings you to Etal and the Black Bull pub.
Parking: Whilst the pub does not have a dedicated car park, there is ample free parking in the village.
Length of the walk: 5½ miles. OS Explorer 339 (GR 928395). There is a single ford to be negotiated.

THE WALK

1 From the **Black Bull** turn right and walk through the village towards the castle, which lies directly ahead. If you would like to look around, the visitor centre contains an excellent and extensive display on the Battle of Flodden which was

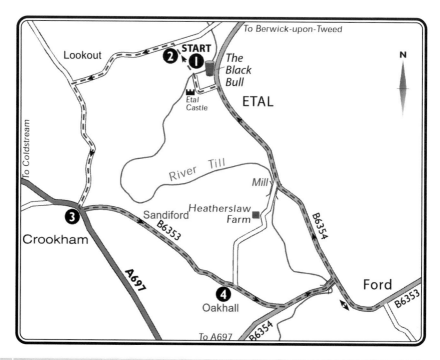

fought nearby (for opening times telephone: 01890 820332).

Turn right by the castle gatehouse and walk down to the ford*. Having crossed the **River Till**, the remains of **St Mary's chapel** will be to the right and you walk straight ahead toward **New Etal**.

* Should the ford prove impassable because of recent rains, retrace your steps from the castle and turn right onto the road leading to Ford. Before you get there, however, take the turn down to Heatherslaw Mill and follow the road to Oakhall. There, turn left again and chase the curve of the road around to the T-junction. Ford castle and village are on your right and, once you've explored these, retrace your steps to the junction and continue on the B6354 back into Etal.

THE 14TH-CENTURY CASTLE AT ETAL.

2 From **New Etal** turn left onto the lane heading west toward **Lookout,** where the track joins the minor road that leads, when you turn left, to the village of **Crookham**. The curve of the **River Till** is to your left as you walk south.

You are now following the line of march of the English army under the Earl of Surrey on the wet morning of 9th September 1513, perhaps 15,000 English marching in battle order toward the Scots army camped on Flodden Edge.

As you enter Crookham, look to your right where the road leads west to Branxton. The stream that meanders by the village is the Pallinsburn and the English turned to cross here and take up their positions at the foot of Branxton Hill facing south. The Scots, alerted by scouts, had massed along the crest of the ridge looking down on the English. The battle began around 4 pm and lasted till dusk. The slaughter was dreadful.

3 At **Crookham** turn left again on the B6353 over **Crookham Bridge** and on through **Sandyford**. Keep going till you reach the left-hand turning onto the very minor road to **Heatherslaw** where you can turn left to visit the mill if you have time (see Place of Interest Nearby).

4 Otherwise, continue along the B6353 and turn left onto the B6354, with the river now on your right till you reach the T-junction. Here turn to your right and the road leads you into **Ford,** with the castle on the rising ground to the left.

The castle, now much altered (and not open to the public), resembles Chillingham in that it comprised four strong towers, linked by sections of stone curtain wall. It was once in the ownership of the Heron family and it is said that Lady Heron beguiled James IV when he occupied the castle before moving on to take up a defensive position on Flodden Edge. A stroll around Ford itself is thoroughly recommended. This is another model village, the building of which was begun by Lady Waterford, circa 1860 and finished by Lord Joicey prior to 1914. Waterford Hall, originally the village school, now functions as a hall and museum.

Once you have enjoyed your look around Ford retrace your steps to the T-junction and bear straight ahead back into **Etal,** passing the manor house on your right.

PLACES OF INTEREST NEARBY

Heatherslaw Mill is a delightfully restored mill complex, the tea room and restaurant provide sustenance and comfort for the weary walker! As an added attraction there is the narrow gauge railway. This runs from April to October 11 am to 3 pm and extending for an extra hour in the afternoons through July and August, then finishing again at 3 pm during September and October. Telephone: 01890 820488.

The Newcastle Hotel

T**HIS IS AN EXHILARATING WALK ON THE HILLS ABOVE ROTHBURY, WITH WONDERFUL VIEWS. THE ROUTE TAKES YOU THROUGH SOME OF THE MAGNIFICENT WOODLAND THAT SWEEPS DOWN THE HILLSIDES AND OUT ONTO OPEN MOORLAND BEFORE RETURNING TO THIS ATTRACTIVE MARKET TOWN.**

Rothbury is situated by the banks of the Coquet and is much frequented by tourists and campers. It is also popular with walkers who roam the nearby Simonside hills. The dark fell sandstone ridge looms above the town which is hemmed by steeply rising slopes north and south. Much of the nearby land to the north forms part of the Cragside Estate. This was created by Victorian industrialist Lord Armstrong, a solicitor turned engineer, whose rifled, breech-loading cannon transformed artillery warfare in the mid-19th century.

THE NEWCASTLE HOTEL is located centrally in the village, next to the parish church of All Saints, overlooking the Lord Armstrong Memorial Cross and the old market place. It is a 19th-century building, of good solid construction in dark sandstone without undue embellishment, and is a comfortable inn, long established and unpretentious. Food is served on Sundays from 12 noon to 5.15 pm and during the week from 12 noon to 2.30 pm, then from 7 pm to 9 pm. Children are welcome and dogs are permitted in the bar area.

☎ 01669 620344.

How to get there: Going north on the A697, at Weldon Bridge bear left at the slip road onto the B6344.

Parking: The pub has no dedicated car parking spaces and though there are few restrictions the town can become crowded at peak times. Generally, the eastern end of the main street is quieter. The pub is centrally situated on the main street.

Length of the walk: 5½ or 6½ miles. OS Explorer 332 (GR 058017). There are some quite steep gradients and do remember that forest pathways can be muddy after wet weather.

THE WALK

1 From the **Newcastle Hotel** cross the main street and ascend to the lane on the higher level that runs parallel and turn left. On the northern flank of the main thoroughfare the ground rises so the shops are located on a lane with a brief interlude of green between the two. Keep walking westwards along the front of the shops till the lane merges and there's a turning to your right that leads uphill toward **Hillside Road**. Follow the steeply climbing lane and turn right at the top onto Hillside Road.

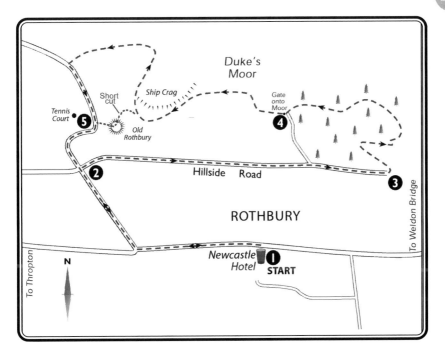

2 You are now heading eastwards, with houses on both sides. Follow the road for about 1½ miles. After the first mile you will pass a left-hand turning but do not take this, keep going till you reach the last of the houses where a wooden sign indicates a footpath through the trees on your left.

3 Follow the path up through the woodland. This is not part of Cragside but belongs to the Duke of Northumberland; you'll pass a marker stone further up. The track is quite clear, it bends to the left and then leads you up a short, steep slope which touches the angle of a stone wall then runs right along the line of the wall. Keep following the path. The way here is clear but can be muddy. After a few hundred yards you come to a much broader, surfaced track. Turn left, going uphill through the trees. The track will gradually bear to the left, westwards, and after walking for several hundred yards

The pleasant market town of Rothbury.

there is an excellent viewpoint by the large stone boulder on your left. This offers a stunning vista of the town and the **Simonsides** beyond. The rock sports a range of incised graffiti, the earliest dating from the Victorian era. After perhaps a mile or so, you arrive at the fringe of the trees and the broad expanse of the **Duke's Moor** opens out in front of you, with **Ship Crag** immediately north-west and the OS marker standing on the high ground to the south-west.

4 Walk over the moor on the track. A wild expanse of heather and bracken stretches north-west over **Debdon**, with **Cartington Hill** almost due north. Past **Ship Crag**, the track veers gradually to the left and then heads northwards.

If you wish to take a short cut back to **Rothbury** at this stage, look for the path on your left that leads from this point directly downhill and through the ramparts of the Iron Age hill fort of **Old Rothbury**. Cross the grassy remains of the ditch and palisade to reach the track that runs back toward the village past the ruined tennis courts. Turn left onto this and continue from point 5.

If you want to walk for a further mile or so in this beautiful countryside, keep on the higher track for ½ mile then take the path to your left that leads you to the larger track running parallel on the lower ground. Turn left onto this and follow it back to the tennis courts.

5 Follow the gravelled road till you reach a gate. Go directly through and then bear right to regain the junction with **Hillside Road**. You now retrace your steps down the bank and back into the town.

PLACES OF INTEREST NEARBY

Cragside, one mile north of Rothbury, was the country house of Lord Armstrong, whose armaments works at Elswick and Scotswood employed tens of thousands of workers in the late 19th century. The house, designed by Anthony Salvin, was the first to have electricity throughout. The unique property and its grounds are currently owned by the National Trust. Telephone: 01669 620333.

The Rose and Thistle

FROM THE HILLSIDE VILLAGE OF ALWINTON, THIS WALK TAKES YOU ON AN ASCENT OF BARROW SCAR AND THEN RETURNS PAST THE SPECTACULAR WATERFALLS OF COQUET GORGE.

Alwinton lies in Upper Coquetdale where undulating farmland gives way to the crowding hills whose tussocky slopes dominate the narrow valley floor below. These are the outriders of the Cheviots that mass toward the high ground of the border. These peaks and valleys were carved by the last Ice Age, which spread deep glaciers over north Northumberland. The church of St Michael is most unusual in that its chancel is higher than the nave, and is reached up a flight of ten steps.

THE ROSE AND THISTLE is an ancient inn, nestling in the fold that the village occupies. It offers a warm and friendly welcome. It would not be difficult to imagine a scene reminiscent of Scott or Thomas Hardy, with the shepherds in their distinctive border plaids gathering around the open fire, tobacco smoke filling the draughty air. Mingling with the hill folk would be cattle drovers, Scots, English and Irish, generally united by a common thirst! It is said that the name derives from a time when the exact border line was not fixed and the pub might call itself English or Scots depending on expediency, an attractive if unlikely explanation!

Food is served from 12 noon to 2.30 pm on Sundays though not on Sunday evenings or at all on Mondays. During the rest of the week the kitchen is open for lunches from 12 noon to 2.30 pm and from 7 pm to 8.30 pm. The fare is typical, good value, bar meals with a range of traditional starters, main courses and puddings. A good selection of beers, spirits and wines are on offer. Children are welcome and dogs are allowed in the bar area.

✆ 01669 650226.

How to get there: From the B6341 turn off west of Rothbury onto a minor road towards Sharperton and continue to Alwinton. The Rose and Crown is centrally situated in the village.

Parking: There is no shortage of free car parking around the pub and in the village car park.

Length of the walk: 4½ miles. OS OL 16 (GR 921064). The route does involve fording the river, which is not deep but will require adequate footwear.

Note: The route passes through an area of land that is occasionally used by the MOD as a firing range. You may not enter whilst the red flag is flying so check the situation beforehand with the range officer by phoning 0191 2394261.

1 From the **Rose and Thistle,** turn left and proceed along the road for some 700 yards till you reach a gate that is marked **Barrow Mill.** Head towards the farm through this gate; pass through a further gate into a field which you cross, passing through yet another gate to reach the river bank. The river is not deep but needs to be forded at this point and, as mentioned, good waterproof boots are therefore essential. Cross the field in front of you and stick with the line of the fence which brings you to yet another gate. Walk toward the derelict farm buildings and stay on the track that takes you to the south-west corner of the wood.

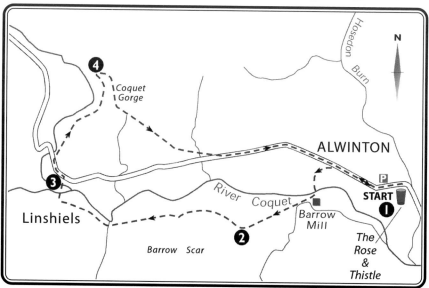

2 You now begin your ascent of **Barrow Scar**, as you skirt the woodland for ½ mile or so. Then, before you reach the range marker, (as mentioned above, this is part of the MoD firing ranges and you may not enter whilst the red flag is flying) take the lesser track over the heather-clad slopes on the right. The ground rises until you reach a fence, the line of which leads over Barrow Scar. When you come to a second fence, walk along this until you reach a stile. Once over this descend towards the bend in the river. You are now heading towards **Linshiels Farm** which will necessitate crossing a further three stiles. Pass through the farmyard, over a pair of bridges and then pick up the road.

3 Turn left for a short distance till you see the sign for **Shillmoor**. Head off up the slope, cross the stile and take the pathway that runs past the **Coquet Gorge** and its attendant waterfalls. As the drop is very sharp, care is needed.

4 Presently you will arrive at a junction. Take the right-hand, higher fork and skirt the crest to join a further track coming in from your left. Turn right onto this path and head uphill. At the gentle summit keep going over the level plateau and then head downhill to the stile. Once over this, keep on the trackway till you come firstly to another stile and then, once again, join the road. Bear left and walk back into **Alwinton**.

PLACES OF INTEREST NEARBY

The area around Alwinton contains a number of interesting prehistoric remains including the excellent hill fort of **Gallow Law.**

The Otterburn Towers Hotel

AN ATMOSPHERIC WALK ACROSS THE MOST RENOWNED BATTLEFIELD IN BORDER HISTORY (1388). FROM THE VILLAGE OF OTTERBURN THE ROUTE TAKES YOU ONTO THE FIELD OF BATTLE AND THEN THROUGH WOODLAND AND PLEASANT COUNTRYSIDE TO RETURN ALONGSIDE THE OTTER BURN ITSELF.

•●•

The contest that was fought during the moonlit night of 19th August 1388 is one of the most renowned in Border history. Sir Henry Percy with a body of men had force marched from Newcastle in the hot summer sun to confront an army of Scottish raiders under the Earls of Douglas and March, laying siege to Otterburn Castle (now the Otterburn Towers Hotel).

Attacking at dusk, the English succeeded in surprising the Scots but the mêlée persisted throughout the night with losses on both sides. A flank attack led by Douglas won the day, though the Earl fell in his moment of triumph. Hotspur was captured and the Scots emerged victorious.

THE OTTERBURN TOWERS HOTEL is a most impressive building with, at its core, the remains of the 14th-century castle the Scots were so keen to reduce in 1388. The setting is unique with pretty gardens to the front and a magnificently panelled dining room. Its restaurant has built up a good reputation locally, and has a comprehensive wine list, supported by a good range of ales and a fine selection of spirits. There is an excellent bar menu offering a selection of traditional fare – on Sundays the pub offers a carvery from 12 noon to 2 pm – lunches are served between the same times during the week and food is also served every evening from 6.30 pm to 7.30 pm. Children are welcome though dogs will have to remain outside.
℘ 01830 520620

How to get there: Otterburn lies on the A696, south of the junction with the A68. Once in the village, the entrance to the Otterburn Towers Hotel is clearly marked.
Parking: There is ample free car parking at the hotel and there is a further car park by the battle memorial.
Length of the walk: 4½ miles. OS Explorer OL42 (GR 887932).

THE WALK

1 Turn right out of the hotel car park and walk through the village. Past the **church of St John the Evangelist,** bear right at the turning for **Otterburn Hall.** This was built in the Tudor style for Lord James Douglas, in 1870 – Lord Douglas

received the land as belated compensation for the death of his ancestor on the field of 1388! Before you reach the hall, however, at the head of the rise from the village, bear left onto the public bridleway, skirt a range of farm buildings and enter a field. Keep with the bridleway till you enter a second pasture. Here you follow firstly, the line of the wall and secondly, the fence to your right.

2 You are now on the field of battle – where you stand perhaps 3,000 Scots and rather more English battled beneath the fitful moonlight over seven centuries ago. Percy's Cross is by the roadside in the small copse to your left. The walk continues over the field, through a gate, and over this next field to a gate set in the far wall. Once through this carry on over the soft ground and pass **Cross Plantation**, much thinned.

3 Turn right on a minor road that wends northward over **Blakeman's Law**. The **Holt** and **Holt Wood** are to your right here. Follow the rising road as it swings to the left over a cattle grid. At the sheepfold, take the footpath that leads off to the right. Once through the gate and past the MoD warning notice follow the path, which may be wet and indistinct in places, downhill. At **Fairney Cleugh** you pick up a better path leading to the right that takes you toward **Hopefoot Farm**, where you will find another metalled road. Bear right, cross the small bridge over the **Otter Burn** and, at **Hopefoot Cottages**, join the road leading from the village to **Otterburn Camp**. You can now return to the village via the road or, as a preferred alternative, pass through the gate you come to on the left opposite the hall drive, which is signposted to **Otterburn**.

4 The footpath leads over a field with the modern sports hall to your right. You will come to a junction of paths by a bend in the fence. Bear left, descending over a couple of

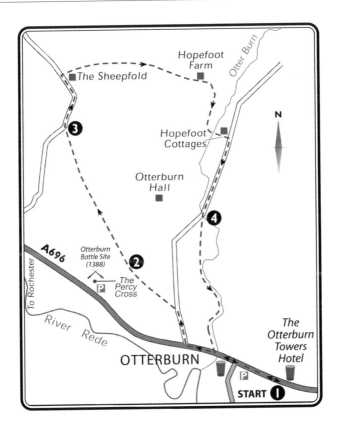

footbridges, through the kissing gate and then along the banks of the **Burn**. Once over the stile you will soon be back in the village. Turn left on the main road to return to the **Otterburn Towers Hotel**.

PLACES OF INTEREST NEARBY

Due north is the village of Rochester which is the site of the Roman fort of **Bremenium**. There is a fascinating Iron Age museum called **Brigantium** which features some remarkable reconstructions of an Iron Age village. Telephone: 01661 886774.

The Riverdale Hall Hotel

THIS WALK TAKES US THROUGH THE HISTORIC TOWNSHIP OF BELLINGHAM, WINDING UPWARDS THROUGH A STEEP AND WOODED VALLEY TO THE BEAUTIFUL WATERFALL AT HARESHAW LINN.

Bellingham is the market town for North Tynedale, one of the upland dales of Northumberland, an unspoilt region brimming with history. The town enjoyed its heyday during the railway era and the North Tyne Line carried on through Falstone to Riccarton Junction on the border with Scotland.

The church of St Cuthbert is Early English, but the 17th-century roof is unique in the county, a fine stone vault with heavy sandstone flags laid in alternating single and double thickness. In the graveyard is the horizontal grave slab known as the Long Pack. A colourful local tale attaches to this: in the 18th century a pedlar called at Lee Hall by Wark and begged the steward of the house to permit him to leave his heavy pack within for the night – he would call to collect it the next morning. The steward was suspicious and kept vigil during the night, his loaded blunderbuss within easy reach. His caution proved justified for in the early hours the pack opened and a boy crawled out. The unknown youth was promptly the recipient of a full load from the blunderbuss and died immediately. It is said that the unlucky lad now rests beneath the Long Pack.

THE RIVERDALE HALL HOTEL is situated just west of the town centre on the Kielder road overlooking the sweep of the North Tyne. Originally a country house it has been a thriving hotel for nearly three decades and has remained in family ownership.

The restaurant service is complemented by a good choice of bar meals including freshly cut sandwiches and a children's menu. A range of traditional beers and lagers is on offer in what is very much a friendly country house, setting. Meals are served in the bar from 12 noon to 2.30 pm and from 5 pm to 9 pm every day. Dogs are allowed in the bar area.
✆ 01434 220254.

How to get there: Bellingham is on the B6320 about 20 miles north of Hexham. As you descend towards the town, almost immediately after the bridge, take the sharp left-hand turning signed for Kielder and the Riverdale Hall Hotel is on your left, 100 yards or so along the road.
Parking: The hotel has an extensive car park.
Length of the walk: 4 miles. OS Explorer OL42 (GR 833834). The walk is not strictly circular as the nature of the trip to the falls necessitates returning by the same route, the valley being narrow and constricted.

THE WALK

1 Leaving the hotel car park turn left onto the road you drove in on and return to the junction. Here bear right (which is effectively straight on) and enter the town with the fire station to your right. By the Council Offices a fortress gun captured from China during the Boxer rebellion stands guard, many thousands of miles from its original home. Walk through the main part of the village street and turn right onto Woodburn Road, before you reach Lloyds Bank. Cross the bridge, then a signpost directs you to the car park for the Linn.

2 As you begin the ascent of the Hareshaw Burn look out for the remains of the Hareshaw ironworks – though only a row of cottages on the east bank and evidence of former spoil heaps remain. The premises opened in 1838 and continued for just a decade. Traces of the dam which served the works

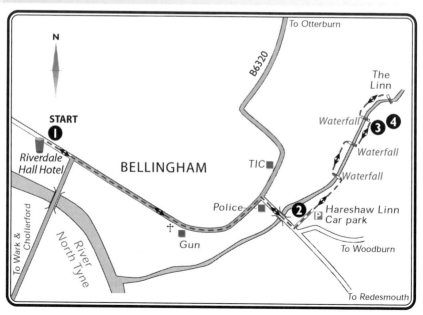

THE FORTRESS GUN FROM CHINA, ON DISPLAY IN BELLINGHAM.

can be discerned further up the Linn. You will also pass the spoil heaps which accumulated from the 70 ovens that used to supply coke to the ironworks. Nearly 500 men were once employed here. The remains of the dam lie beyond and the peaceful flow of the burn belies its occasional ferocity: the last serious flood was in 1968. The valley is steep-sided and densely wooded and has been designated as a Site of Special Scientific Interest, teeming with wildlife and a rich diversity of mosses and lichen.

As you progress you pass over the remains of an earlier quarry which yielded stone for the local houses and you can make out the entrances to several blocked-up mine shafts. Past the mine shafts, the hill to your left was a favourite place for rolling pace eggs at Easter. Once through the kissing gate you're into the Linn proper. Past the curved stone seat you come upon **Cupid's Bower** – past the second bridge traces of two more abandoned mine shafts are visible.

3 From the third bridge proceed to the fourth. Here the area is planted with Douglas firs, a legacy of the Victorians. We also have them to thank for the footpath which leads us now over the fifth and sixth bridges. Traces of a bandstand, another Victorian creation, carved from the hillside, face you as you cross the sixth bridge. **The Linn** itself is a steep-sided waterfall formed by the constant pressure of water, eroding the soft sandstone over millennia. The place abounds with some 300 species of mosses, liverworts and lichens, some of which are virtually unique to this habitat. It is a magical place, timeless and enclosed.

4 From **the Linn** retrace your steps to the car park. The Heritage Centre located 200 yards further up Woodburn Road in the former station yard is well worth a visit.

PLACES OF INTEREST NEARBY

The dale was settled in prehistoric times and many Iron Age settlements survive; a good example is preserved at **Tower Knowe**, on the shores of Kielder Reservoir by the information centre. This can be found approximately 6 miles north-west of Bellingham. Telephone: 01434 240398.

The Hollybush Inn

A WALK ON MINOR ROADS THROUGH THE WILD MOORLAND AROUND THE HAMLETS OF GREENHAUGH AND TARSET, ACCOMPANIED BY THE AMBLING WATERS OF THE BURNS THAT RUN THROUGH THE VALLEYS. THE REMAINS OF TARSET CASTLE ARE A REMINDER OF HOW WILD THIS AREA ONCE WAS.

◆●◆

Greenhaugh is deep in reiver country and a number of peles or bastles stud the area. These stout, double-storied, stone blockhouses are a far cry from the great coastal castles. Four-square, squat and functional, the masonry is crude but massive. They were built strictly for the business of defence with no pretence to grandeur. The ground floor is usually stone vaulted, the better to resist efforts to smoke out or 'scumfish' the defenders on the upper level. Beneath was reserved for the precious livestock, sturdy black cattle and sheep whilst the family occupied the chamber above.

THE HOLLYBUSH INN is a long, low, typically Northumbrian building, ancient in appearance but probably dating from the 18th century. The exterior can have changed very little in that time. Within, it is as you would expect, with rustic bead and butt latched doorways, roughcast plaster, low ceilings and the cheer of open fires. There is a traditional no-nonsense bar with separate dining area. Meals are served during the evenings only on Tuesdays, Wednesdays and Thursdays from 7 pm to 9 pm and in the dining room also on Fridays and Saturdays, also from 7 pm to 9 pm. Sunday lunches are offered from 12 noon to 2 pm. There is no food at lunchtime on weekdays. Children are welcome and dogs are permitted in the bar area only.
⌀ 01434 240391.

How to get there: Greenhaugh is on a minor road between Bellingham on the B6320 and Kielder Water. The pub is on the left as you drive through the village.
Parking: There is parking opposite the pub.
Length of the Walk: 5 miles. OS Explorer OL42 (GR 794873).

THE WALK

1 As you leave the Hollybush, turn right and walk through the village. Almost immediately the road begins to climb with woodland on the right. You will pass the entrance to Greenhaugh Hall, buried in the trees. As you top the rise there is a turning to your left to Otterburn but proceed directly ahead, the road levelling out and passing Brownknowe and Snow Hall. The road now takes you past the WI hut to the crossroads at Lanends. Here turn right

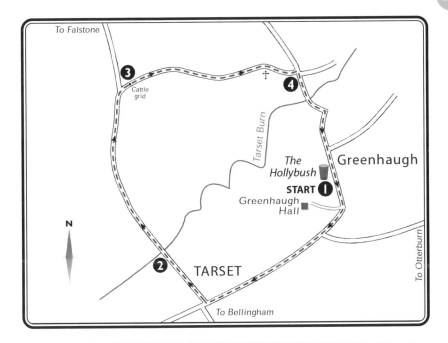

into Tarset, following the lane downhill to the charming little 19th-century bridge at Redmire. The Tarset Burn runs along the valley floor, the brown waters ambling over glassy boulders. At the bottom of the incline, above the burn, stand the remains of Tarset Castle. What survives is the stump of the motte which was defended by a ditch around the base.

2 Over the bridge and you're heading west, climbing again. Just before you reach the cattle grid, the remains of an Iron Age settlement can be identified on your right on the flank of Boggle Hill. At the cattle grid the road separates, the turning on your left is to Rushend and Thorneyburn but you keep to the right onto the track that leads over the line of the ridge.

3 The Lairney Burn runs in the small valley on the left and the Seat is on the right. You next come to another right-hand

THE VIEW TOWARDS THE COMBE NEAR GREENHAUGH.

turning and you follow this as it dips toward Thorneyburn Lodge, the church and rectory. Pass the church on your right – the grouping, with the rectory, stables and surrounding walls is typical of Seward's work. As you continue your descent toward the T-junction the Tarset Burn flows past the plantation on the right.

4 When you reach the junction turn right and follow the road to Burnmouth, crossing the Tarset Burn. Continue back into Greenhaugh village, passing the school on your left.

PLACES OF INTEREST NEARBY

Nearby is the bastle or pele house at **Black Middings** which is in the ownership and care of English Heritage. The building is well preserved, though roofless. There is a small car park at the foot of the slight rise that it occupies and access is all year round.

The Milecastle Inn

H ERE IS A WALK ALONG A DRAMATIC SECTION OF THE ROMAN
WALL BUILT BY THE EMPEROR HADRIAN, WITH UNSPOILT
COUNTRYSIDE ALL AROUND AND SPECTACULAR VIEWS IN EVERY
DIRECTION.

———————●●●———————

The B6318 is General Wade's military road build in the 18th
century to confound rebellious Jacobites. Wade was a prolific
builder of military roads and most of his work was carried out
in the Scottish highlands in an effort to deter the rebel clansmen.
This now runs parallel to a rather earlier work of military
engineering. The Roman wall was built at the direction of the
Emperor Hadrian in about AD 122–128. This is the central
section of the great wall where it strides along the basalt outcrop
of the whin sill, a natural defensive barrier. A milecastle was a

small fort located every Roman mile (roughly 1,000m). It housed a small garrison of perhaps a dozen men and between each were two stone towers or turrets intended as permanent lookouts and which would be home to two or three men.

THE MILECASTLE INN is a long established roadhouse with a restaurant that offers an excellent à la carte selection of local dishes. There is also a range of bar food with the daily fare being written up on blackboards. Typically this includes the usual favourites such as a range of steak options, Cumberland sausage, chicken and a distinctive variety of game pies. A children's menu is available and a good choice of puddings and coffee. An excellent wine list is on offer, together with a range of traditional hand-pulled ales. Food is served usually from midday to 2.30 pm and then from 6 pm to 9 pm. Dogs are welcome.
✆ 01434 321372.

How to get there: The Milecastle Inn is located on the B6318 approximately 15 miles west of Chollerford and 3 to 4 miles east of Greenhead at the Haltwhistle/Cawfields crossroads. **Parking:** The car park is to the rear of the inn. There is also parking at Cawfields picnic area where there are picnic tables and well maintained WCs (locked from end October-Easter). **Length of the walk:** 4 miles. OS Explorer OL43 (GR 916688). Sensible outdoor clothing is advised.

---

① Leaving the pub car park, cross the long straight arrow of General Wade's military road. Follow the sign to Cawfields picnic area and car park. The picnic area covers the site of a former quarry and the sheer cliff face, which chops off a section of the Roman wall, is a legacy of this industrial past.

② Follow the footpath along the north side of the lake to

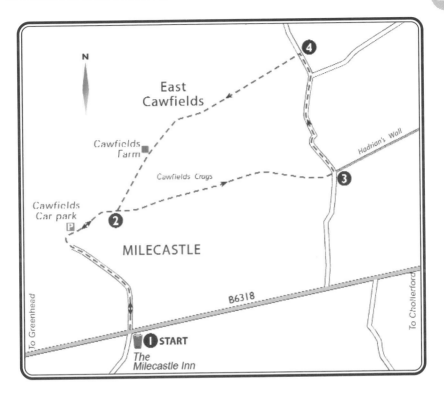

where it snakes around the sheer cliff to bring you out, through a gate, onto the line of the wall itself. You are almost immediately confronted by the remains of Cawfields Milecastle, the walls standing chest high with both of the original gateways clearly identifiable. This gives a very good idea of the size of these small outposts, situated every Roman mile. You are now on the south side of the great wall looking northward over the sweeping moorland of Henshaw Common, Black Fell, Thirlwall Common and Spadeadam Waste. To the south the view extends over Plenmeller Common to Cross Fell and the dark mass of the northern Pennines, limestone country replacing the fell sandstone. Now walk eastwards along the line of the wall by the footpath, which is punctuated by a series of short but

CAWFIELDS MILECASTLE ON HADRIAN'S WALL.

steep declines and rises. Steps are provided. As you walk along Cawfields Crags, the line of the wall begins to rise. Ahead of you is the highest point at Winshields. You pass turrets 41 B and A, before reaching the dip in the path and the road intersection near Bogle Hole.

3 Leave the line of the Wall and follow the narrow road north, until you reach the track on the left leading to East Cawfields.

4 Follow this until you pass through Cawfields Farm and arrive back at the picnic site. Retrace your steps back to the Milecastle Inn.

PLACES OF INTEREST NEARBY

Travelling east along the Military Road (B6318) stands the impressive Roman fort at **Housesteads** (Borcovicium). There is a small museum on site. Telephone: 01434 344363.

The Hadrian Hotel

A WALK THAT OFFERS A FASCINATING STRETCH OF HADRIAN'S WALL AND THE SITE OF AN EPIC 7TH-CENTURY BATTLE, WITH WONDERFUL VIEWS AND WOODLAND PATHS, BEFORE RETURNING TO ONE OF TYNEDALE'S MOST PICTURESQUE VILLAGES.

Wall is a pretty village with the church and a number of stone-built houses grouped along a wide green set, not surprisingly, not far from Hadrian's Wall. Some of the older properties undoubtedly began life as bastles (fortified houses) though of the 'terrace' type. Its seems odd to us that such stout defensible constructions should appear in terraces, as though forming part of a modern streetscape. These are distinguished by having their byre and upper level doors located in the long front wall rather than in the gables as we see in 'detached' bastles. The walk takes us by St Oswald's church nearby which marks the location of the epic battle of Heavenfield in AD 635, when Oswald of Northumbria rescued his Christian kingdom from the ravages of Cadwallon, a pagan Welsh prince, destroying his army and leaving the Welshman dead on the field.

THE HADRIAN HOTEL is a busy wayside inn and enjoys splendid views over the Tyne valley. The pub has a large range of ales, wines and spirits, and has been established as a first-class restaurant for many years. The bar menu is extensive and covers the usual fare of traditional meat, game and fish dishes, with a good choice of starters and puddings, and a children's menu is available. Food is served daily from 12 noon to 8.30 pm. Dogs are permitted in the bar.
✆ 01434 681232.

How to get there: Wall lies between Chollerford and Hexham in the valley of the South Tyne. The Hadrian Hotel is located on the A6079 as it passes through the village on the western flank of the extensive green.
Parking: The car park for the pub is plainly visible and free of charge to patrons.
Length of the Walk: 4 miles or 1½ miles. OS OL43 (GR 916688).

THE WALK

1 Cross the road from the pub car park and take the lane directly opposite. Carry on past the 'No Through Road' sign, leaving the new housing behind, and pass the vicarage. Follow the track you're now on as it bears left and begins to ascend. Pass through a metal gate marked as a bridleway and then continue on the path. Where this, in turn, bears left, follow the lesser track which veers more to the right

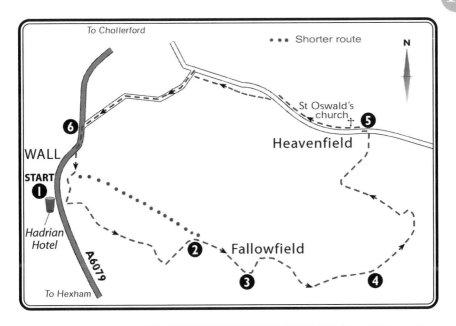

over a field. You now come to a wicket gate, with a small wooded area on your right.

2 Turn right through the gate till you reach another in the angle of the field. Proceed along what appears to be an ancient walled trackway. The masonry should stay on your left as you arrive in another field. Stay on the track, another wicket gate awaits in the top corner. Once through this gate look out for a post on your left.

For the shorter walk, branch off at the post and, veering left, go over a stone stile into a wood. Once through the trees and over another stile you come to a stretch of open moorland. A further post is visible ahead, make directly for this. The path, well defined, which leads from the post takes you to another stone stile. Once over this bear left, down through a field with the wall of a wood on your right. A right turn at the angle of the wall brings you to a further stile and the directional arrow will lead you into an Iron Age

St Oswald's cross marks the site of the
Battle of Heavenfield in AD 635.

hill fort. The descent from the area of the settlement is quite
steep and may be slippery in wet weather but the village is
clearly visible before you. Go down a set of steps onto the
playing field toward the road, where a left-hand turn brings
you nearer Wall. Follow the route back over the village
green as given in 6 below.

To continue on the longer walk, pass this and carry on
toward the cottage and wooded area before you. Climb a
stone stile into the trees and follow the path. Now turn right
and then left at the junction, this is Fallowfield. Fallowfield
Fell once yielded sandstone for the building of nearby
Hadrian's Wall. Some ancient graffiti survived as one group
of Roman engineers left an ad hoc inscription PETRA
FLAVI CARANTI, 'the rock of Flavius Carantius' (now in
Chester's Roman Fort museum).

3 Pass a set of barns and farm buildings and then bear to your right on another track – this will be signed 'Public Bridleway Salmonswell 1½'. Stay on the track, passing through a couple of gates. Then, 200 hundred yards or so further on, turn off the track onto a path on your left which is marked as a public footpath. Keep going along here. Pass through another gate with tall pines to the right, and keep the trees on your right till you spy a series of rocky outcrops on your left.

4 Pass through the next gate you come to, then bear immediately left. The path here is less well marked but the fence should remain on your left until it begins to veer away. Then look out for a small hillock or mound which lies to your right and you will come to a waymarker post. At this junction keep to your left, cross over the wooden stile and proceed some 50 yards to yet another marker post. Continue left, uphill to a third post. You will now be on the brow of the plateau and will need to turn right onto a farm track. Follow this to a gate, pass through and you'll be on a minor road which is also waymarked.

5 The wooden cross which marks the site of the battle of Heavenfield and Oswald's standards in AD 635 is ahead of you. Cross the road, passing the display boards, and go through the gate, angling left toward a wall. Take a sharp left and the end of this wall brings you to a ladder stile – this now places you on Hadrian's Wall National Trail. Keep with the trail, the ditch on your left, over a further three stiles till you arrive back at the main road. Cross this, go over another stile and continue right. Carry on across the field to yet another stile and stick with the trail. This now takes you over two more stiles, through woodland onto a further minor road which you follow for ½ mile. The slope you descend is **Brunton Bank** and features a short but most fascinating stretch of **Hadrian's Wall**. Here you can see the spot where the 'broad' wall (some 10 ft in width) heading west meets the 'narrow' wall some 4 ft thinner, which continues down toward Brunton Turret. This is a remarkably fine example and very prettily located.

6 At the main road turn left. Cross the junction with a minor road, then take the next left towards the village. When you reach the T-junction bear right and take the road that leads you over the green, leaving the **Methodist chapel** (from 1868) on your right. At the next T-junction you again bear right to return to the pub.

PLACES OF INTEREST NEARBY

As you drive westwards along the Military Road, dipping down to the roundabout just over Chollerford Bridge, there is a sign on your left, as you approach the bridge, that marks the footpath to the bridge abutment opposite **Chesters Roman Fort**. This is a delightful short walk of a few hundred yards which leads to the foundations of the original **Roman Bridge** and offers a view of the fort opposite.

The Lord Crewe Arms Hotel

THIS IS A WALK AROUND THE DELIGHTFUL VILLAGE OF BLANCHLAND ON THE BANKS OF THE DERWENT. THE ROUTE TAKES YOU ALONG AN OLD DROVE ROAD TO SHILDON, LEADING OVER THE HIGH SWEEP OF BLANCHLAND MOOR BEFORE BRINGING YOU BACK INTO THE VILLAGE.

●●

Blanchland's streets and square, constructed in mellow local sandstone, are particularly pretty, the village nestling amongst the crowding hills. The abbey was founded in 1175 by the then lord of the manor Walter Bolbeck and suffered frequently at the hands of marauding Scots; it was Henry VIII, however, who was responsible for its dissolution in 1539. In the 18th century, the property came into the possession of the Crewe Trustees, who were responsible for building the present settlement, incorporating such elements of the old monastic church as had survived.

THE LORD CREWE ARMS, in the centre of Blanchland, is an imposing building and was originally the west wing of the monastic complex. It has a long established reputation as a hotel and the interior décor reflects its historic pedigree. In addition to an excellent restaurant menu and wine list, bar food and sandwiches are available. The restaurant has two great open fires and long, sweeping windows, with superb views of the Durham hills, while portraits of Lord Crewe and his wife Dorothy still gaze down upon today's diners. Food from the extensive bar menu is served daily from 12 noon to 2 pm and then from 7 pm to 9 pm. Children are welcome and dogs are permitted in the bar area.
☎ 01434 675251.

How to get there: From Hexham follow the B6306 southward, signposted for Slaley and Blanchland.
Parking: It is possible to park more or less outside the hotel, otherwise there is a 'pay and display' car park adjacent to the village square.
Length of the walk: 3½ miles. OS OL31 (GR 968505).

THE WALK

① Leaving the Lord Crewe Arms, walk up through the square and toward the north-west corner, passing a rather delightful ladies' hat shop before you pick up the track which heads off to your left. This is, in fact, a former drove road. Northumberland can boast a network of these historic roads which had their heyday in the 18th and 19th centuries

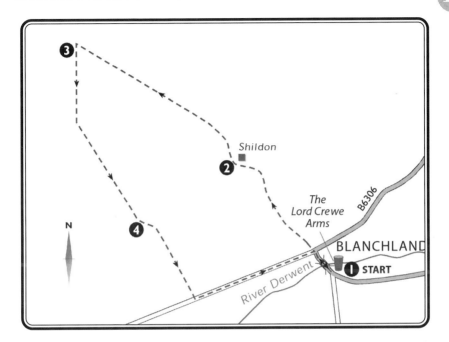

when Scots and local drovers herded their charges to markets in the south. The Shildon Burn flows prettily on the left and after about ½ mile you come to what remains of the settlement at **Shildon**.

2 This was a lead mining centre from the medieval period until the seams were finally exhausted in the 19th century. The building, known locally as Shildon Castle, began life as an engine shed constructed in the prevailing Cornish style, with a distinctive tall stack beside it, an interesting remnant of the area's industrial past. Walk on past Shildon, with the burn still on your left and the rising ground of Pennypie Fell to your right. Continue for almost 1 mile to Pennypie House.

3 Turn sharply left to head south-east towards Stothill Plantation. The ground to your left, above and south of the burn, retains traces of numerous mine shafts.

4 Take the right-hand fork of the track at Stothill plantation and walk into the hamlet of Baybridge. Immediately across the River Derwent into County Durham is the charming village of Hunstanworth. This was largely remodelled in an attractive, almost Arts and Crafts style by the Victorian architect S. S. Teulon in 1862–1863 and the houses on the Northumbrian side echo his style. Nearby on the Durham side is Dead Friars Hill. It is said that Scottish raiders, having sought out the White Canons abbey at Blanchland, became lost in fog as they traversed the bleak moorland above. As they emerged, lost, on the Durham side they distinctly heard the sound of the bells ringing to celebrate the monks' supposed deliverance from their attentions. Alerted by this obliging peal they tracked the sound till they came upon the monastery and put the unwise brothers to the sword! Turn left on the road back into Blanchland.

PLACES OF INTEREST NEARBY

Despite the strongly rural character the area was, in previous centuries, quite heavily industrialised with lead being mined nearby. Two heritage mine sites at **Killhope,** near Cowshill, (telephone: 01388 537617) and **Nent,** near Alston, (telephone: 01434 382037) offer a fascinating glimpse of this lost heritage.

The Angel Inn

From the attractive town of Corbridge, this walk takes us towards Dilston, on the bank of the Tyne, and to the ruins of the last and tragic Earl of Derwentwater's fine and extensive mansion. We then return to the start past the Devil's Water, one of the most romantic places in the county.

• • •

Corbridge was originally a Roman supply base and the remains of Corstopitum lie just to the west by the old back road to Hexham. The village, which is one of the most attractive in Tynedale, has a fine church and an adjacent Vicar's pele, a reminder of the centuries of border wars when the local clergy were enthusiastic participants! It is well furnished with cafés, bistros, specialist shops and a good-sized tourist information centre.

THE ANGEL lies on the north side of the river, before the magnificent span of the bridge. It is a fine building that occupies a commanding position on the main street and inside there is a cosy interior with a timber-panelled dining area. The bar/restaurant is reminiscent of a classic country pub with low ceilings and timber fittings throughout. It offers an excellent restaurant and a comprehensive bar menu comprising traditional meat, fish and game dishes. Food is served daily from 12 noon to 2.30 pm and from 6 pm to 9 pm (except Sundays). Children are welcome and dogs are allowed in the bar.

☎ 01434 632119.

How to get there: Corbridge lies on the A69, Newcastle to Carlisle road. Arriving from Tyneside in the west, the Corbridge exit road brings you into the southern flank of the town. The Angel is on your right once you've passed the garage.

Parking: There is ample car parking by the pub itself and a large free public car park on the south side over the bridge.

Length of the Walk: 4 miles OS OL43 (GR 993644). The climb from Dilston to the Devil's Water, though stepped, can be slippery in wet or wintry conditions.

THE WALK

1 Leaving the Angel, turn right, then cross the street to reach the bridge over the Tyne. Once across bear left onto the minor road and walk toward the station, which will be on your left. Pass over the railway crossing and bear left toward a Y-junction. Here, you turn right onto the A6080 – this will lead you, after somewhat less than 1 mile, into the hamlet of Dilston New Town. Stay with the left-hand fork which, after a further ½ mile, brings you in sight of Dilston Hall and Castle.

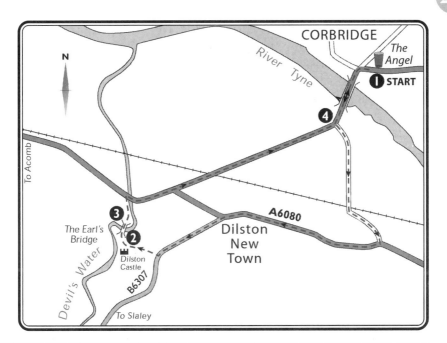

The Hall dates from around 1835 and was constructed from stone salvaged from the earlier and much larger house. The building is presently occupied by a mental health charity as a training centre but the castle and adjacent chapel are open to the public during the spring and summer season. There is an admittance charge and café and toilet facilities on site (telephone 01434 382037 for further details).

The castle is all that stands of the magnificent Jacobean mansion of the Earl of Derwentwater. The chapel which faces you as you look toward the castle is of particular interest as it is a unique example of a post-Reformation recusant (Catholic) chapel. It is said to have been built by Sir Francis Radcliffe, who may have been the shadowy mastermind behind the Gunpowder Plot.

2 Having passed the castle on your left, you will see that the

land dips sharply down toward the Devil's Water. There is a path with steps which leads you through the tangled and overgrown ruin of Dilston Hall's terraced gardens down to the stream. This is one of the most romantic locations in the county. The burn flows over rocks through tree-crowded banks – watch out, for you may catch sight of the ghost of the countess as she mourns her husband! The bridge, which dates from 1621, is particularly elegant, rising in a single elliptical span over the Devil's Water.

3 Pass directly over the bridge and follow the track through a scout camp. When you come to a minor crossroads, go straight ahead till you rejoin the road linking Hexham to Corbridge. Turn right toward Dilston itself and then follow the arrow-straight road as it heads back toward Corbridge. Dilston Haughs is on your left and you cross the railway once again.

4 When you arrive at the Y junction just before the bridge, turn sharp left. Once you've crossed the bridge, take time to explore the town a little more. Proceed uphill for 150 yards or so and then bear left toward the charming market square. The cross which dominates the tidy square dates from 1814. The church and the Vicar's pele are on your right. The parish church of St Andrew is regarded as one of the most significant surviving Saxon monuments in the county (the crypt of Hexham Abbey being the other). Retrace your steps back to the Angel.

PLACES OF INTEREST NEARBY

Aydon Castle is just to the north, along the appropriately-named Aydon Road from which it is signposted. The monument, in the care of English Heritage, is a superbly preserved 14th-century fortified manor house, which was continuously occupied until the late 1960s. Telephone: 01434 632450.